CHARLOTTE HARTWELL

Adulting For Anxious Young Adults

Life Skills to Manage Stress, Conquer Anxiety, and Live Confidently

Contents

III PART 3: ESSENTIAL LIFE SKILLS

Introduction

Welcome to your personal guide to adulting! This book is your trusty road-map as you navigate the sometimes daunting, often exhilarating journey into adulthood. Think of it as your go-to resource—you don't have to read it cover to cover. Instead, explore the chapters that resonate with you, whether you're tackling a new responsibility or just looking for helpful tips.

Transitioning into adult life can feel like a whirlwind. There's so much to learn, and it often seems like you're expected to know everything already. Unfortunately, many of the crucial life skills needed to thrive as an adult—like managing finances, navigating social dynamics, and taking care of your mental health—aren't taught in school. That's where this book comes in. It's designed for young adults like you who are eager to learn the ropes of adulthood but may feel overwhelmed by all that's expected of you.

While this book won't provide all the answers, it offers practical guidance to help you figure things out. From moving out on your own to managing your finances, it's all here, ready for you to explore. Whether you're learning how to cook, mastering time management, or understanding how to build healthy relationships, this book is packed with the kind of advice that will make your transition into adulthood a little smoother.

As I reflect on my own journey into adulthood, there are countless things I wish I had learned sooner. Moving out for the first time was overwhelming—figuring out where to live, managing rent, and handling the logistics of moving on my own were all major challenges. Suddenly, grocery shopping wasn't just a quick trip; it became a strategic mission to stay within budget. And don't even get me started on taxes. The first time I tackled them alone, it felt like trying to decode an ancient language.

One of the biggest lessons I've learned is that you never stop growing. Each stage of life brings new responsibilities, and the key is to approach these challenges with an open mind, stay curious, and keep trying. Persistence is your best friend. Develop a routine, and eventually, it will become second nature.

Why this book is for you

If you're navigating the complexities of adulthood, this book is designed with you in mind. Adulthood can be overwhelming, especially when you're dealing with anxiety or neurodivergent learning challenges. Whether your interests lie in video games, spending time with animals, crafting, or journaling, you'll find practical advice that fits your lifestyle.

Anxiety is more than just a feeling of nervousness or worry—it's a powerful force that can affect every aspect of your life. When anxiety takes hold, it can hijack your brain, making even the simplest tasks feel overwhelming. The brain's fight-or-flight response kicks in, flooding your body with stress hormones like cortisol. This reaction, while helpful in dangerous situations, can be counterproductive in everyday life, leading to a state of

2

chronic stress.

When anxiety is persistent, it can cloud your judgment, making decision-making and problem-solving more difficult. Your brain might focus on worst-case scenarios, trapping you in a cycle of worry that leads to procrastination. Instead of tackling tasks head-on, you might find yourself avoiding them altogether, which only increases your anxiety in the long run. This avoidance can create a vicious cycle, where the more you delay, the more overwhelming the tasks become, and the more anxious you feel.

Anxiety doesn't just make things harder—it can make you believe that you're not capable. It can convince you that the challenges of adulting, like managing finances or living independently, is overwhelming. This book offers strategies to help you approach these responsibilities with confidence, breaking them down into manageable steps that reduce stress.

Neurodiversity is a term that celebrates the natural variations in the human brain. It acknowledges that not everyone thinks, learns, or processes information in the same way. Neurodiversity encompasses a range of conditions, including ADHD, autism, dyslexia, and more. These conditions aren't deficits—they're different ways of experiencing the world.

For those with neurodivergent learning differences, traditional advice often doesn't fit the way you process information, which can lead to frustration and a feeling of being misunderstood or unsupported. This book recognizes that one size does not fit all, especially when it comes to learning and personal development.

It offers tailored solutions that align with your learning style, whether it's mastering time management, handling workplace interactions, or navigating social situations. The guidance here is practical, compassionate, and designed to help you build routines that work for you.

Managing finances, dealing with taxes, or paying off debt can be particularly stressful when coupled with anxiety or neurodivergence. This book simplifies these processes, offering clear strategies to help you take control of your financial life without feeling overwhelmed.

Workplace dynamics can also be a source of anxiety, especially in environments that don't always cater to neurodiverse needs. This book provides insights on how to communicate effectively, advocate for yourself, and create a work environment that supports your well-being, ensuring that you can thrive professionally while staying true to yourself.

This isn't just a guide—it's a companion on your journey through the ups and downs of adulting. It's here to help you build a life that aligns with your values, supports your mental and emotional health, and celebrates your unique strengths. Together, we'll tackle the challenges of adulthood, empowering you to step into this new chapter with confidence and resilience.

I

Part 1: THE BASICS OF ADULTING

Chapter 1: Embracing Independence

Leaving the Nest

Leaving the nest conjures images of baby birds spreading their wings for the first time, tentatively fluttering into the great wide open. For humans, the transition to independent living is no less momentous, often feeling more like a leap into the unknown than a gentle flight. You're not just stepping out of your parents' house; you're stepping into a new chapter of your life, one that promises both freedom and responsibility. As daunting as it may seem, embracing independence is a rite of passage that can be incredibly rewarding.

Coping with the Fear of Leaving Home

Let's be honest: the idea of leaving home can be terrifying. You're moving away from the familiar comforts of home-cooked meals, laundry done for you, and, perhaps most importantly, the emotional safety net of having family close by. It's perfectly normal to feel apprehensive. In fact, a study by the Pew Research Center found that 36% of young adults in the U.S. were living at home with their parents in 2020, the highest number since the Great Depression. Many cited economic uncertainty and the fear of taking the plunge into independence as key factors.

But fear, while natural, shouldn't be paralyzing. Break down this massive life change into manageable steps. Start by acknowledging your fears and writing them down. Are you worried about managing finances? Concerned about feeling lonely? Identifying these fears is the first step in addressing them.

Consider Sarah, a recent college graduate, who felt overwhelmed by the prospect of living alone. She worried about everything from cooking meals to paying bills. Instead of letting these fears consume her, she decided to tackle them head-on. She took a basic cooking class, which not only taught her essential skills but also boosted her confidence in the kitchen. She also set up a budgeting app to track her expenses, ensuring she stayed on top of her finances. By facing her fears directly, Sarah found that they were far less daunting than they initially seemed.

Steps to Ensure a Smooth Transition to Independent Living

Once you've identified your fears and started addressing them, it's time to plan your transition. Think of this process as a project, with a timeline, tasks, and milestones. Here are some practical steps to help ensure a smooth transition:

1. **Financial Preparation:** Before you move out, make sure you have a financial cushion. Experts recommend having at least three to six months' worth of living expenses saved up.

This safety net will give you peace of mind as you navigate the initial costs of moving out and setting up your new place.

2. **Find the Right Place: Find the Right Place:** Choosing where to live is crucial. Look for a location that fits your budget and meets your needs in terms of proximity to work, public transportation, and social activities. Start by exploring the best rental websites specific to your location to find comprehensive listings and detailed information. Additionally, consider using Facebook Marketplace, which is becoming a popular platform for finding rental listings. It offers the added benefit of seeing mutual friends with landlords or other tenants, adding a layer of trust to the process.

3. **Understand the Basics of Renting:** Familiarize yourself with lease agreements, rental insurance, and tenant rights. Knowing what you're signing up for can prevent future headaches.

4. **Set Up Utilities and Services:** Once you've secured a place, set up essential services like electricity, water, internet, and gas. Many utility companies offer bundled services, which can save you money.

5. **Furnish Gradually:** You don't need to have a fully furnished apartment from day one. Start with essentials— bed, kitchen basics, and a place to sit—and gradually add items as your budget allows.

How to Choose Where to Live

Choosing where to live is one of the most significant decisions you'll make. It's not just about finding a roof over your head; it's about creating a space where you can thrive. When searching for your new home, don't settle for the first place you see. It's important to visit multiple listings to compare options and get a feel for what's available within your price range. Here are some factors to consider:

- **Budget:** Your rent should ideally be no more than 30% of your monthly income. Don't forget to factor in additional costs like utilities, groceries, transportation, and entertainment.
- **Location:** Proximity to work or school can significantly impact your quality of life. A longer commute can mean less time for yourself and higher transportation costs. Additionally, consider the safety and amenities of the neighborhood.
- **Roommates:** Living with roommates can be a great way to reduce costs and combat loneliness. However, it's crucial to choose compatible roommates. Discuss expectations around cleanliness, noise, and shared responsibilities before moving in together.
- **Amenities:** Decide what amenities are important to you. Do you need a pet-friendly place? A gym in the building? On-site laundry facilities? Make a list of non-negotiables and nice-to-haves.

Embracing Independence

The journey to independence is as much about self-discovery as it is about practicalities. It's an opportunity to learn more about yourself—what you value, how you handle challenges, and what kind of life you want to build. It's about taking ownership of your life and making decisions that align with your goals and values.

Leaving the nest is a significant milestone that marks the beginning of an exciting new chapter. It's a journey filled with challenges, but also immense opportunities for growth and self-discovery. By breaking down the process into manageable steps, addressing your fears, and making informed decisions, you can navigate this transition with confidence and grace. Remember, independence is not about doing everything perfectly—it's about taking control of your life and learning along the way.

Chapter 2: Financial Literacy

Money: it's one of those things we all need but often dread dealing with. You might have heard the saying, "Money can't buy happiness," but let's be real—it can certainly buy peace of mind. Understanding financial literacy is like having a superpower. It gives you control over your future, reduces stress, and opens up opportunities. So, let's dive into the world of budgeting, saving, and debt management with a little humor and a lot of practical advice.

Financial Independence

Achieving financial independence is like mastering a video game. At first, you might be clueless, pressing random buttons and hoping for the best. But with practice, you get better, make smarter moves, and eventually, you're the boss of your finances.

Start by tracking your income and expenses. It might sound tedious, but it's the foundation of financial literacy. Think of it as a real-life version of managing resources in "The Sims." You wouldn't let your Sim blow all their Simoleons on a fancy couch if they couldn't pay their bills, right? Similarly, knowing where your money goes helps you make informed decisions.

Anecdote: Take Jamie, for example. After college, Jamie landed a decent job but felt broke all the time. It turns out, Jamie was spending a small fortune on takeout coffee. By tracking expenses, Jamie realized cutting back on those lattes could save nearly $1,000 a year. That's a vacation fund right there!

Basic Budgeting: The Magic of Planning

Creating a budget is a lot like planning a road trip. Think about it: you wouldn't set off on a long journey without knowing your starting point, your destination, and the best route to get there. The same principle applies to managing your money. A good budget balances your needs, wants, and savings, guiding you smoothly from where you are now to where you want to be financially.

First things first, list your income. This is like figuring out where your gas money is coming from for that big road trip. Include your salary, any freelance work, side gigs, and other sources of money. Don't forget about taxes—consider them the toll roads of your financial journey. No one likes a surprise tax bill, so it's crucial to account for these deductions right from the start. We'll dive deeper into taxes later, but for now, just know they're a part of your budgeting road-map.

Next up, it's time to track your expenses. Think of this as mapping out your pit stops along the way. You have fixed expenses, like rent and utilities—these are your non-negotiables, the essential stops you can't avoid. Then, there are variable expenses, like groceries and entertainment—these are the scenic detours and roadside attractions that make the journey enjoyable. Be honest with yourself here; pretending those weekend outings and spontaneous online shopping sprees don't exist won't make them disappear. Knowing where every dollar goes helps you plan your trip more accurately and avoid unexpected detours.

Now, let's talk about setting savings goals. This is your ultimate destination, the beautiful place you want to reach by the end of your journey. Aim to save at least 20% of your income. I know, it sounds ambitious. But even if you start with 5% and gradually increase, you're making progress. Each dollar saved is a mile closer to your goal. Think of it like this: your savings are your emergency roadside assistance, the funds you can rely on when the journey gets rough, like a flat tire or a surprise engine problem.

Budgeting is all about making conscious choices and prioritizing your future self. Ramit Sethi, author of "I Will Teach You to Be Rich," says, "Spend extravagantly on the things you love, and cut costs mercilessly on the things you don't." This might sound counterintuitive, but it's about prioritizing joy in your spending. Identify what truly brings you happiness and what doesn't, then adjust your budget accordingly. If those daily lattes are your little slice of heaven, keep them. But maybe cut back on something that doesn't add much to your life. This approach makes budgeting feel less like deprivation and more like intentional living.

A Beginner's Guide to Filing Taxes

Taxes: the word alone can send shivers down your spine. But they don't have to be a nightmare. Think of taxes as a civic duty—like voting, but with more paperwork. To make filing taxes easier, it's important to prepare throughout the year. Here's a simple way to get started:

Know Your Status: Are you single, married, or head of household? Your filing status affects your tax rate.

Set Aside Money for Taxes: If you're self-employed or have a side gig, it's smart to set aside about 25-30% of your income for taxes. This way, you're not caught off guard when tax season rolls around. You can use a separate savings account to keep this money safe.

Track Your Income and Expenses: Keep a record of all your income and expenses. There are many apps that can help with this, like QuickBooks or even a simple Excel spreadsheet. Tracking everything helps you see where your money goes and what you might owe in taxes.

Stay Organized & Save Receipts: Create a folder (physical or digital) where you can keep all your tax-related documents. This includes receipts, invoices, and any forms you receive, like W-2s from your job. Having everything in one place makes it much easier when it's time to file.

Get Help from Professionals: If taxes feel too complicated, don't worry. You can get help from professionals. Services like

H&R Block or TurboTax can make the process easier. If your taxes are really complicated, think about hiring an accountant.

Paying Off Debt: Slaying the Financial Beast

Debt is like a heavy backpack on a hike—it slows you down and makes the journey harder. But with a plan, you can lighten the load.

1. **List Your Debts:** Include student loans, credit cards, and any other debts. Note down the interest rates and minimum monthly payments for each. This gives you a clear picture of what you owe.
2. **Prioritize Your Debts:** Focus on paying off high-interest debt first. This is often called the "avalanche method." By tackling the debts with the highest interest rates first, you save money on interest over time. Another approach is the "snowball method," where you pay off the smallest debts first to gain quick wins and build momentum. Choose the method that keeps you motivated.
3. **Make Extra Payments:** Whenever possible, pay more than the minimum. Even a little extra each month can make a big difference over time. Extra payments go directly to the principal balance, reducing the total amount of interest you'll pay.
4. **Use Windfalls Wisely:** If you receive unexpected money, such as a tax refund, bonus, or gift, consider putting it towards your debt. It might be tempting to splurge, but paying down debt is a gift to your future self.
5. **Cut Unnecessary Expenses:** Review your budget and iden-

tify areas where you can cut back. Cancel unused subscriptions, eat out less often, and look for cheaper alternatives for your regular expenses. Redirect the money you save towards paying off your debt.

The Importance of Credit Scores and How to Improve Yours

Your credit score is like your financial reputation. It's a three-digit number that tells lenders how risky it is to lend you money. A good score opens doors to better interest rates on mortgages, loans, and credit cards, while a bad score can close them. So, how is this number determined, and how can you improve it? Credit scores usually range from 300 to 850 and are calculated based on several factors, including your payment history, amounts owed, new credit, and even the length of your credit history. Importantly, credit can be built not just by using credit cards but also by consistently paying your recurring bills such as mobile contracts and other financial responsibilities. Now that you understand what factors contribute to your credit score, here are some practical tips to help you improve it.

1. **Check Your Score:** Regularly review your credit report for errors. Use free services like Credit Karma or annualcreditreport.com to keep tabs on your credit.
2. **Pay Bills on Time:** Always pay your bills on time. Set up automatic payments or reminders to avoid missing due dates.
3. **Reduce Credit Card Balances:** Aim to keep your credit card

balances below 30% of your credit limit. Paying down debt is crucial for a healthy score.

Improving and building your credit is a gradual process, but with consistent effort and responsible financial behavior, you can achieve a strong credit score. This opens up many financial opportunities, from lower interest rates on loans to better terms on mortgages and credit cards. So take control of your credit today and set the stage for a financially secure future.

Anecdote: Maria ignored her credit score until she was denied a car loan. After checking her score, she realized several late payments and high credit card balances were the culprits. By paying bills on time and reducing her balances, she improved her score and eventually got that car loan with a favorable interest rate.

Saving Money

Building an Emergency Fund and Beyond

Having savings is like having a safety net. It catches you when life throws unexpected expenses your way. Imagine it as a financial cushion that softens the blow of life's unpredictable moments—job loss, medical emergencies, or sudden car repairs. But how do you build this safety net, and what steps should you take beyond that?

Let's start with the basics: an emergency fund. This fund is your financial security blanket, meant to cover three to six months' worth of living expenses. Yes, it might seem like a daunting amount, but the peace of mind it brings is priceless. Think of it as paying yourself first. Every time you get paid, set aside a portion of your income directly into a separate savings account, something small that does not drastically alter your lifestyle. Automating this process is key. If you don't see the money, you won't miss it, and your savings will grow effortlessly over time.

This fund is for true emergencies, like job loss or medical bills, not for that tempting sale at your favorite store.

Once you have a solid emergency fund, it's time to think about other savings goals. Maybe you're dreaming of a vacation, a down payment for a house, or even early retirement. For these goals, it's essential to understand where your money goes and find ways to save more. Review your budget regularly. Are there subscriptions you no longer use? Dining out less frequently can also make a big difference. Every dollar saved is a dollar closer to your dreams.

Earning extra income through a side hustle can also accelerate your savings. Whether it's freelancing, dog walking, or selling handmade crafts, any additional income can be funneled into your savings. The more you save, the more opportunities you open up for yourself in the future.

Investing is another powerful way to grow your savings. Start with something simple, like a high-yield savings account or a retirement account. As you become more comfortable, consider diversifying your investments with stocks, bonds, or mutual funds. The key is to start small and educate yourself along the way. The earlier you start investing, the more time your money has to grow.

Let's not forget the wisdom of Dave Ramsey, who famously says, "Live like no one else now, so later you can live like no one else." It's about making smart, sometimes tough choices today to enjoy financial freedom tomorrow. Maybe that means cooking at home instead of dining out or choosing a staycation over a lavish trip. These sacrifices, however small they might seem, compound over time to create significant savings.

Mastering financial literacy is an ongoing journey, not a one-time event. By tracking your income and expenses, creating a budget, understanding taxes, managing debt, and building savings, you're setting yourself up for financial success. Remember, it's okay to make mistakes—what's important is learning from them and staying committed to your financial goals.

Financial independence isn't about being rich; it's about having the freedom to live the life you want without financial stress. So, take control of your money, make informed decisions, and watch as your financial future unfolds with promise and potential.

II

PART 2: PERSONAL GROWTH AND WELL-BEING

Chapter 3: Time Management and Organization

Time management and organization might sound like topics straight out of a corporate training seminar, but they are essential life skills that can transform your daily routine from chaos to calm. Think of your life as a complex video game with multiple levels and challenges. Whether you're trying to balance work, social life, hobbies, or self-care, mastering time management and organization can make a huge difference.

Prioritizing Tasks

Creating to-do lists that work: The Eisenhower Matrix

Ever feel like you're constantly putting out fires but never making progress on the things that really matter? Enter the Eisenhower Matrix, a simple tool that helps you prioritize tasks based on urgency and importance. Named after President Dwight D. Eisenhower, this matrix can help you decide what to work on first, what to delegate, and what to ignore.

Here's how it works:

- **Urgent and Important**: These are the tasks that need your immediate attention. Think of them as the boss fights in your video game. You can't ignore them; you need to tackle them head-on. Examples include meeting work deadlines, attending critical meetings, or dealing with emergencies.
- **Important but Not Urgent**: These tasks are crucial for your long-term success but don't require immediate action. These are your level-up opportunities—working on a personal project, studying for a certification, or planning future goals. Schedule these tasks to ensure they get the attention they deserve.
- **Urgent but Not Important**: These tasks demand your attention now but don't significantly contribute to your long-term goals. They're the mini-bosses—annoying but manageable. Examples include answering non-critical emails, attending some meetings, and handling minor issues. Delegate these tasks if possible.
- **Not Urgent and Not Important**: These are the time-wasters. Avoid them like traps in a game. Scrolling through social media, binge-watching shows, and unnecessary internet surfing fall into this category. Limit these activities to your downtime to ensure they don't eat into your productive hours.

Mastering your Schedule

With your tasks prioritized, the next step is to master your schedule. One powerful technique to manage your time is **Time Blocking**. Imagine dividing your day into blocks of time, each dedicated to a specific task or group of tasks. For instance, you might dedicate the first two hours of your workday to high-priority projects—your boss fights. Then, allocate the next hour to responding to emails and messages, those necessary but less critical side quests.

Another effective strategy is the **Pomodoro Technique**. Named after the tomato-shaped timer, this method involves working for 25 minutes, then taking a 5-minute break. After four cycles, you take a longer break of 15-30 minutes. This technique helps maintain focus and energy, ensuring you don't burn out before completing your mission.

In this digital age, **Digital tools** are your best allies. Apps like Google Calendar, Todoist, or Trello are fantastic for keeping track of your schedule and tasks. They can send reminders, help you set deadlines, and provide a visual representation of your day. Think of them as your in-game inventory, keeping all your items (tasks) organized and accessible. With these tools, you'll never forget a crucial deadline or miss an important meeting.

Decluttering Your Space and Mind

Ever feel like the clutter in your space is creeping into your mind, making it hard to focus and relax? You're not alone. A cluttered environment can lead to a cluttered mind. But don't worry; with a few simple strategies, you can create a more organized and peaceful space.

Tips for Maintaining an Organized Living Space

Let's start with the physical clutter. Imagine your living space as your personal sanctuary—a place where you can relax and recharge. Keeping it organized doesn't have to be a monumental task. Here are some tips to help you maintain an organized living space:

- **Start Small:** Begin with one area at a time. Maybe it's your desk, a kitchen drawer, or your closet. Tackle it bit by bit, so you don't feel overwhelmed. Just like in a video game, you wouldn't try to complete every quest at once; you'd focus on one mission at a time.
- **Declutter Regularly:** Make it a habit to go through your things regularly. Donate or discard items you no longer need or use and keep only the essentials. This can be a monthly ritual.
- **Create Storage Solutions:** Invest in storage bins, shelves, and organizers to give everything a designated place. Label these storage solutions to make it easy to find what you need. If you're looking for creative storage ideas, browsing Pinterest can provide plenty of inspiration.
- **Daily Tidying:** Spend a few minutes each day tidying up. Put things back where they belong, clean up surfaces, and keep your living space neat. By dedicating just a small portion of your day to tidying up, you can prevent clutter from building up and turning into a daunting, time-consuming task. When you tidy up daily, it keeps your environment manageable and also means you spend less time on big cleaning projects, freeing up your weekends and giving you more time to enjoy your hobbies and relax. Plus, it creates a

more pleasant and productive atmosphere. In short, a few minutes of tidying each day can make a big difference in maintaining a calm, orderly living environment.

Digital Decluttering

Next, let's talk about your digital space. Your computer and phone can get cluttered just like your living room. Here's how to keep your digital life organized:

Organize Files: Create a folder system that makes sense to you. Group similar files together and name them clearly. Regularly delete files you no longer need. By keeping your files organized, you can quickly find what you need and maintain a streamlined workflow.

Email Management: Unsubscribe from newsletters you don't read and delete old emails. Use folders or labels to organize important emails. This not only reduces digital clutter but also makes it easier to locate important messages when you need them.

Clear Your Desktop: A cluttered desktop can be distracting. Keep only the files and shortcuts you use frequently. Move everything else into appropriate folders. A clean desktop can improve your focus and efficiency, making your daily tasks more manageable.

Mental Decluttering Techniques

Just as a tidy room can improve your physical environment, a clear mind can significantly enhance your mental state. Mental clutter—those persistent thoughts, worries, and distractions— can weigh you down and hinder your ability to focus, create, and enjoy life fully. By learning to declutter your mind, you can achieve greater clarity, tranquility, and overall well-being. Let's explore some effective methods to help you streamline your thoughts and bring a sense of order to your mental landscape.

Mindfulness Meditation: Close your eyes. Breathe in deeply, then exhale slowly. Spend a few minutes each day practicing mindfulness. Sit quietly, focus on your breath, and let your thoughts come and go without judgment. This simple practice can transform your day, grounding you and bringing clarity to your thoughts. According to a study published in the Journal of the American Medical Association, mindfulness meditation can reduce anxiety, depression, and pain. Jon Kabat-Zinn, a pioneer of mindfulness-based stress reduction, says, "You can't stop the waves, but you can learn to surf." It's like pressing pause on life's chaos and taking a moment to center yourself.

Journaling: Grab a notebook and let your thoughts spill onto the page. Write down your feelings, dreams, worries, and triumphs. Journaling is more than just a diary—it's a tool for processing emotions and clearing mental clutter. A study by the University of Texas at Austin found that expressive writing can boost immune function and reduce stress. Think of it as a personal sanctuary where you can reflect on your journey and celebrate your achievements.

To-Do Lists: Ever feel overwhelmed by the sheer volume of tasks swimming around in your head? Write them down. Keeping a running list of tasks and priorities helps you stay organized, reduce anxiety, and ensure nothing slips through the cracks. Plus, there's something deeply satisfying about crossing items off your list.

Limit Information Overload: In today's digital age, we're bombarded with information every second. Be mindful of how much you consume. Take regular breaks from social media and the news. Give your mind the rest it desperately needs. A study from the University of California, Irvine found that it takes an average of 23 minutes to refocus after a distraction. It's like stepping away from a noisy crowd into a quiet, peaceful room. You'll be amazed at how much more focused and refreshed you feel.

Balancing Responsibilities: Juggling Work, Social Life, and Personal Projects

Life is a bit like juggling, isn't it? You've got work in one hand, social life in the other, and personal projects floating somewhere in between. Keeping all these balls in the air can feel like a never-ending circus act. But don't worry; with the right strategies, you can become a master juggler.

An important habit to learn is **setting boundaries**. It's crucial to clearly define your work hours, social time, and personal project time. Let your friends and family know when you're available and when you need to focus. This way, you can give your full attention to each aspect of your life without feeling pulled in a million directions.

Sometimes, you have to learn the art of saying no. It's not about being rude; it's about being realistic. If your schedule is packed and someone asks you to take on another task or attend another event, it's okay to decline. You can't carry everything, so you need to be selective about what you pick up. Saying no to less important things means you have more energy for what truly matters.

Communication is critical. Keep open lines of communication with your boss, colleagues, friends, and family. Let them know your limits and when you're available. This way, they understand and respect your time.

Then there's the importance of **scheduling downtime**. Yes, you heard that right. Make sure to schedule regular breaks and activities that relax and rejuvenate you. Whether it's reading, playing video games, or spending time with loved ones, downtime is essential for maintaining your overall well-being.

Finding balance is also about being **flexible and adaptable**. Life is unpredictable, and sometimes you'll need to switch up your plans. Maybe a work project takes longer than expected, or a friend needs support. Being able to adapt without feeling stressed is key.

Technology can be your ally here too. Use calendar apps to block out time for different activities, ensuring you don't double-book yourself or neglect any area of your life. Set reminders for breaks, and use task management tools to keep track of your personal projects.

Lastly, give yourself some grace. Not every day will be perfectly balanced, and that's okay. Some days, work might take up more time, while other days, you might focus more on personal projects or social activities. The key is to find a rhythm that works for you, understanding that balance isn't about perfection—it's about making adjustments and finding harmony over time. So grab your calendar, set your priorities, and get ready to juggle like a pro!

Chapter 4: Workplace Confidence

Navigating Workplace Anxiety

Entering the professional world is like stepping onto a stage where the spotlight can be both exhilarating and intimidating. The transition from college or an entry-level job to a more defined career path often brings a mix of excitement and anxiety. However, this stage—with its challenges and opportunities—is where you begin defining your professional identity. Navigating workplace dynamics, managing anxiety, and building a career you love are crucial steps to gaining confidence and thriving in your twenties and beyond.

Understanding workplace dynamics and how to fit in

Understanding workplace dynamics is like learning a new language. Every office has its own culture, unspoken rules, and social nuances. To fit in and excel, you need to become fluent in this new environment. Start by observing and listening. Pay attention to how colleagues interact, the flow of communication, and the decision-making process. Who holds informal power?

What values seem to guide the team? Contributing to a psycho-logically safe environment can significantly reduce workplace anxiety and foster a more inclusive and productive atmosphere.

Techniques for managing anxiety at work

Workplace anxiety is common, but it can be managed. The first step is to recognize it and find ways to keep it under control. One effective approach is to reframe your thoughts. For example, if you're nervous about a presentation, try to focus on the opportunity to share your ideas rather than on the fear of making mistakes.

Regular exercise can also help reduce anxiety. A study by the American Psychological Association shows that activities like taking short walks, stretching, or practicing mindfulness during breaks can make a big difference. It's important to take care of your mental health, not just your workload.

Another powerful way to manage anxiety is by embracing vulnerability. Dr. Brené Brown, a research professor at the University of Houston, explains that vulnerability involves having the courage to be open and honest, even when you can't control the outcome. She says, "Vulnerability is not winning or losing; it's having the courage to show up and be seen when we have no control over the outcome." By allowing yourself to be vulnerable, you build stronger connections with others, which can provide much-needed support and reduce feelings of anxiety. Combining physical activity with emotional openness creates a more balanced and resilient approach to handling workplace stress.

Building a Career You Love

Identifying your passions and aligning them with career opportunities.

Building a career you love starts with introspection. What are you passionate about? What activities make you lose track of time? Identifying your passions isn't always straightforward, but it's a crucial step. Reflect on your interests, skills, and values. Consider seeking guidance from mentors or career coaches who can provide insights and help you see possibilities you might not have considered.

Once you've identified your passions, work on aligning them with career opportunities. This doesn't necessarily mean making a dramatic career change. Sometimes, it's about finding ways to incorporate your interests into your current role or seeking out projects that excite you. As Steve Jobs famously said, "The only way to do great work is to love what you do. If you haven't found it yet, keep looking. Don't settle."

Decision Making

Making career decisions can feel overwhelming, but it's important to approach them with a clear mind and strategic thinking. Start by gathering information. Research potential roles, companies, and industries. Speak to professionals in those fields to get a realistic picture of what to expect.

Next, weigh your options carefully. Consider the pros and cons, and think about how each choice aligns with your long-term goals. Will it bring you closer to your dream career, or steer you away from it? Think about the potential benefits and drawbacks, not just for now, but for the future as well.

However, don't stop there—trust your instincts too. Sometimes, the best decisions come from a gut feeling rather than a detailed analysis. Malcolm Gladwell, in his book *Blink: The Power of Thinking Without Thinking,* talks about the power of our initial reactions. Our subconscious often picks up on subtle cues that our conscious mind overlooks. It's like having a hidden radar that senses the right direction even when things seem unclear.

Imagine you're standing at a crossroads. One path looks logically perfect, filled with opportunities that align neatly with your plans. But there's another path that tugs at your heartstrings, igniting a spark of excitement and curiosity. That's your gut speaking. Maybe it's a job offer that doesn't quite match your skill set on paper, but something about it feels right. Or perhaps it's a project that scares you a bit but also thrills you. Don't ignore these feelings.

Combining logic with intuition can be a powerful way to make decisions. Weigh the facts, listen to advice, analyze the risks, but also pay attention to how you feel. After all, you're the one who will walk this path, and it needs to resonate with who you are and where you want to go.

Growth Mindset, Self-Confidence, and Resilience

A growth mindset, as described by psychologist Carol Dweck, is the belief that abilities and intelligence can be developed through dedication and hard work. Embracing this mindset can transform how you approach challenges and setbacks. Instead of seeing them as failures, view them as opportunities to learn and grow. "In a growth mindset, challenges are exciting rather than threatening. So rather than thinking, 'Oh, I'm going to reveal my weaknesses,' you say, 'Wow, here's a chance to grow,'" says Dweck.

Building self-confidence is a gradual process. Start by setting small, achievable goals and celebrating your successes, no matter how minor they seem. Confidence grows from recognizing your accomplishments and learning from your experiences.

Workplace confidence isn't about never feeling anxious or making mistakes. It's about navigating these challenges with a sense of purpose and resilience. Resilience, the ability to bounce back from setbacks, is essential. It's about how you handle tough times and come out stronger. Here are three key strategies to help you stay strong:

1. **Accept That Suffering Is a Part of Life:** Everyone faces challenges and difficulties, and it's normal to experience setbacks. Understanding this helps you not feel alone in your struggles
2. **Choose Where to Focus Your Attention:** Instead of dwelling on negative thoughts or problems, try to concentrate on positive aspects and what you can control.

This shift in focus can make a big difference in how you feel and act.

3. **Assess Whether Your Thoughts Are Helping or Hurting You:** When you catch yourself thinking negatively, pause and consider if that thinking is useful. If it's not, try to shift your perspective to something more positive and constructive.

By using these strategies, you can stay grounded and keep moving forward, even when things don't go as planned. Resilience helps you handle life's ups and downs with more confidence and strength.

Chapter 5: Neurodiversity and Learning

Embracing Neurodiversity

Neurodiversity is a concept that recognizes and respects the variety of human brains and minds. It's about understanding that differences in how we think and learn are not deficiencies, but unique strengths. Embracing neurodiversity means acknowledging these differences and finding ways to thrive with them. Whether you have ADHD, dyslexia, autism, or any other neurodiverse condition, understanding your learning style and finding effective strategies can make a world of difference.

Understanding Neurodiverse learning complications

Neurodiverse individuals often face unique challenges in both learning and working environments, and these challenges can significantly impact daily life. For instance, someone with ADHD might find it difficult to focus and stay organized, while a person with dyslexia may struggle with reading and writing tasks. Recognizing these difficulties is the first crucial step toward finding effective strategies to overcome them.

But how do you know if you're neurodiverse? Common signs include persistent difficulties in areas like attention, reading, writing, or social interaction that differ from typical developmental patterns. For example, if you've always found it exceptionally hard to concentrate on tasks, frequently lose track of time, or feel like your mind is constantly buzzing with distractions, you might have ADHD. Similarly, if reading has always been a slow, laborious process despite your efforts, dyslexia could be a factor. These challenges often appear early in life and continue into adulthood, affecting how you navigate both personal and professional spaces.

Take ADHD, for example. Individuals with ADHD often struggle with executive function, which includes skills like planning, focusing, and managing time. Traditional time management techniques, like making to-do lists or setting strict schedules, might not work because they don't account for the unique challenges of sustaining attention or avoiding distractions. This can make tasks that seem simple to others feel overwhelming and frustrating.

Autistic individuals might face different but equally significant challenges. Social interactions and sensory environments can be overwhelming, making it difficult to navigate the workplace or public spaces comfortably. The way they process information might be more detail-oriented or hyper-focused on specific interests, which can be a tremendous strength in the right environment but a challenge in others. This focus can lead to exceptional expertise in certain areas, but it can also make transitioning between tasks or adapting to new situations particularly stressful.

Dyslexia, on the other hand, affects how people process language, making reading and writing more difficult. Traditional approaches to learning, which often emphasize reading and writing as the primary modes of acquiring knowledge, might not accommodate these differences. This can lead to struggles in educational and work settings, where these skills are often taken for granted.

A formal diagnosis from a healthcare professional, such as a psychologist or neurologist, can provide clarity. They use various assessments and tools to determine whether your experiences align with neurodiverse conditions. While getting a diagnosis can feel daunting, it's a crucial step in understanding your unique brain and learning how to best support it.

It's important to remember that these learning challenges aren't a reflection of your intelligence or capability. Instead, they highlight the need for different approaches and tools. Dr. Thomas E. Brown, a clinical psychologist who specializes in ADHD, explains, "Neurodiverse individuals often possess incredible strengths, such as creativity, problem-solving skills, and the ability to think outside the box. The key is to harness these strengths while addressing the challenges."

Understanding and embracing your neurodiversity can open doors to new strategies and resources that make life's tasks more manageable. Whether it's finding alternative ways to manage your time, learning how to communicate more effectively in social situations, or discovering tools that make reading and writing easier, recognizing and working with your unique strengths can help you thrive.

Strategies for effective learning and working as a Neurodiverse individual

Developing effective strategies tailored to your unique brain can transform your learning and working experiences. Different neurodiversities require different approaches, so let's explore some practical tips to help you succeed:

ADHD: Managing Focus and Time

Break Tasks into Smaller Steps: For individuals with ADHD, large projects can feel overwhelming and lead to procrastination. Breaking tasks down into smaller, manageable steps makes it easier to start and stay focused. For example, instead of tackling an entire research paper at once, break it down into steps like choosing a topic, outlining, and writing one section at a time.

Set Clear Goals and Deadlines: ADHD often makes it difficult to stay on track without clear objectives. Establishing specific, achievable goals and setting firm deadlines can help maintain focus and motivation. Using tools like planners, calendars, or apps that send reminders can be particularly helpful in keeping track of tasks and deadlines, helping you maintain a steady and productive pace.

Take Regular Breaks: Individuals with ADHD might struggle with maintaining focus over long periods. Techniques like the Pomodoro Technique—where you work for 25 minutes and then take a 5-minute break—can help sustain energy and prevent burnout. Regular breaks allow your mind to reset, making it easier to return to the task with renewed focus.

Autism: Creating Order and Reducing Sensory Overload

Create a Structured Environment: For autistic individuals, a structured and predictable environment can reduce anxiety and increase productivity. Setting up a designated workspace that is free from clutter and interruptions can help maintain focus and reduce sensory overload. This might include using noise-canceling headphones or minimizing bright lights to create a more comfortable environment.

Use Visual Aids: Autistic individuals often excel with visual learning. Visual aids like charts, diagrams, and color-coded notes can help organize information and make complex concepts easier to understand. For example, using a visual schedule can break down daily tasks and routines, making them more manageable and less overwhelming.

Set Clear Goals and Deadlines: Establishing clear expectations can be especially beneficial for those who thrive on routine and structure. Setting specific goals and realistic deadlines helps create a sense of order and ensures you know exactly what needs to be done and when.

Dyslexia: Enhancing Learning Through Alternative Methods

Use Visual Aids: Dyslexia can make processing written information challenging, but visual aids can bridge that gap. Diagrams, charts, and color-coded notes can help dyslexic individuals organize and digest information more effectively. For example, mind maps can be a useful tool for organizing thoughts and ideas before writing.

Break Tasks into Smaller Steps: For those with dyslexia, large reading or writing tasks can be daunting. Breaking them down into smaller steps can make the process more achievable. Instead of reading a whole chapter at once, try tackling it one section at a time, taking notes as you go.

Seek Feedback and Adjust: Regular feedback is crucial for individuals with dyslexia to understand what strategies are working. Be open to trying new methods and adjusting your approach as needed. This flexibility can help you find the most effective ways to learn and work.

General Strategies for All Neurodiversities

Take Regular Breaks: Regardless of your specific neurodiversity, taking regular breaks is important to prevent burnout and maintain productivity. It's essential to listen to your body and mind, giving yourself the time to rest and recharge.

Seek Feedback and Adjust: Neurodiverse individuals benefit greatly from regular feedback. This allows you to identify what strategies are effective and where adjustments are needed. Being flexible and open to change is key to finding what works best for you in different learning and working environments.

By tailoring these strategies to your specific needs, you can create an environment that supports your learning and working style, helping you thrive both personally and professionally.

Finding Support

Resources and Communities for Neurodiverse Individuals

Finding the right support can make a significant difference if you think you might be neurodiverse. Whether you're certain or just suspecting, there are plenty of online and offline communities ready to welcome you with open arms. Websites like ADDitude, Understood.org, and the Autism Society offer a wealth of resources, including insightful articles, active forums, and support groups where you can connect with others who understand your experiences.

Joining these communities isn't just about finding information—it's about finding a sense of belonging. Imagine being part of a group where people understand your unique challenges and strengths. You can share stories, swap tips, and receive advice that resonates with your experiences. It's a place where you can feel seen, heard, and accepted. So, dive in and explore these resources—you'll discover you're not alone on this journey.

How to ask for accommodations at work and school

Asking for accommodations can be daunting, but it's crucial for your success. First, familiarize yourself with your rights. Many countries have laws requiring schools and employers to provide reasonable accommodations for individuals with disabilities. Understanding these regulations can give you confidence when making your request. Whether you're in Europe, Australia, or elsewhere, knowing your rights ensures you can advocate for the support you need.

Next, be prepared. Before you approach anyone, take some time to figure out exactly what you need. Think about how your neurodiversity affects your work or studies and what specific accommodations would make a difference. Having a clear idea will help you communicate more effectively.

When it's time to have the conversation, be direct and specific. Explain your situation, how it impacts your performance, and what accommodations would help. For example, you might say, "I have ADHD, which makes it hard to concentrate in noisy environments. A quieter workspace would really help me stay focused."

If you're unsure how to start, don't hesitate to seek support. Talk to a trusted advisor, counselor, or HR representative. They can offer guidance and help you navigate the process. Sometimes, having someone in your corner can make all the difference.

Remember, follow-up is key. After you've made your request, check in regularly to ensure the accommodations are being implemented and are working for you. If there are any issues, don't be afraid to speak up and suggest adjustments.

Asking for accommodations might feel intimidating, but it's a vital step in creating an environment where you can thrive. With the right support and strategies, you can turn your unique challenges into strengths.

III

PART 3: ESSENTIAL LIFE SKILLS

Chapter 6: Cooking and Nutrition

Basic Cooking Skills

Essential kitchen tools and pantry staples.

Cooking is an essential life skill that can save you money, improve your health, and boost your confidence. Whether you're whipping up a quick breakfast before work or preparing a cozy dinner for friends, knowing your way around the kitchen is incredibly empowering.

Imagine this: You've just decided to cook your first homemade meal. You're excited, ready to channel your inner chef. But then you realize you don't have the right tools or ingredients. Don't worry—we've all been there. Here's a guide to stocking your kitchen with the essentials.

Every aspiring cook needs a few basic tools. These are the building blocks of your culinary adventures:

- **Chef's Knife:** This is your kitchen workhorse, perfect for chopping vegetables, slicing meat, and dicing herbs. Invest in a good one, keep it sharp, and it will serve you well for years.

· **Cutting Board:** Choose a sturdy wooden or plastic one that's large enough to handle everything from chopping carrots to carving a roast.

· **Mixing Bowls:** A set of mixing bowls in different sizes is crucial. They're useful for mixing, marinating, and even serving. Stainless steel bowls are durable and easy to clean.

· **Non-Stick Skillet and Saucepan:** These versatile pieces of cookware can handle everything from frying eggs to simmering sauces. Add a baking sheet for roasting vegetables and baking cookies, and you're set.

· **Smaller Tools:** Don't forget the essentials like measuring cups and spoons for accuracy, a vegetable peeler, and a spatula. These might seem minor, but they make cooking much easier.

Pantry Staples

Now, let's talk about pantry staples. These are the ingredients you should always have on hand to create a variety of dishes. Start with olive oil and vegetable oil. Olive oil is great for salad dressings and sautéing, while vegetable oil is perfect for frying and baking. Salt and pepper are must-haves. They're the foundation of seasoning. Add garlic and onions to the mix, and you have the basics for flavoring almost any dish. Keep a selection of dried herbs and spices. Basil, oregano, cumin, and paprika can elevate your meals with minimal effort.

Rice and pasta are versatile and filling. They're perfect bases for a variety of meals. Canned beans and tomatoes are also great to have. They're convenient, nutritious, and can be used in countless recipes.

Simple, healthy recipes for beginners.

Now that your kitchen is stocked, let's get cooking! When you're just starting out, it's best to keep things simple and build your confidence with a few tried-and-true recipes. Think about dishes like a vibrant vegetable stir-fry, a hearty chicken pasta, creamy homemade hummus, or versatile oven-roasted vegetables. These meals are not only easy to make but also packed with nutrients.

For inspiration, there are plenty of resources available online. Websites like BBC Good Food, Epicurious, and AllRecipes offer a wide array of simple, healthy recipes perfect for beginners. YouTube channels like Tasty and Binging with Babish provide visual guides that can make the cooking process feel less intimidating and more fun. The great thing about YouTube is that it caters to different learning styles and paces. You can pause, rewind, and rewatch videos as many times as you need, ensuring you grasp each concept fully before moving on. Plus, seeing the final dish come together can be incredibly motivating and inspiring.

Cooking doesn't have to be complicated. With the right tools, a well-stocked pantry, and a few simple recipes, you can create delicious, healthy meals with ease. Remember, the key is to start small and build your confidence in the kitchen. As you become more comfortable, you'll find joy in experimenting and trying new things.

Meal Planning and Preparation

Meal planning and preparation can be a game-changer in your daily life. It not only saves time and money but also helps you eat healthier and reduce food waste.

Planning your meals for the week might sound daunting, but with a little organization, it can become a straightforward and even enjoyable task. Here's how to get started:

- **Assess Your Schedule**: Start by looking at your week ahead. Identify the days you'll have time to cook and the days you might need something quick and easy. Are there nights you'll be out or days you might need to pack lunch? Knowing your schedule helps you plan accordingly.
- **Choose Your Recipes**: Select a mix of recipes that fit your week's needs. Include a variety of proteins, vegetables, and grains to keep things balanced. Websites like BBC Good Food, Epicurious, and AllRecipes offer an array of ideas. Look for recipes that share ingredients to make shopping easier and more cost-effective.
- **Create a Meal Calendar**: Write down what you'll be eating each day. This can be on a physical calendar, a whiteboard, or a digital planner. Seeing everything laid out helps ensure you're covering all meals and snacks without overcomplicating things.

- **Prep in Advance**: Dedicate some time, perhaps on the weekend, to prep your meals. This can involve chopping vegetables, marinating proteins, or cooking grains. Prepping in advance can significantly reduce the time spent cooking on busy weekdays. Imagine opening your fridge to find ready-to-cook ingredients waiting for you—life just got a lot easier!

Tips for Efficient Grocery Shopping

Efficient grocery shopping goes hand-in-hand with meal planning. Start by making a detailed list based on your meal plan, dividing it into sections like produce, dairy, and pantry items to streamline your shopping trip. Before heading to the store, check what you already have to avoid buying duplicates and make use of what you already own. For staples like rice, pasta, beans, and spices, buying in bulk is usually cheaper and ensures you have plenty on hand for future meals.

When at the store, stick to the perimeter where fresh produce, meats, dairy, and bakery items are typically located. This helps you make healthier choices. Also, don't shop on an empty stomach to avoid impulse buys and unhealthy choices. Lastly, stay flexible with sales and seasonal produce. If you find a great deal on chicken thighs or see that zucchinis are in season and cheap, adjust your meal plan accordingly. Seasonal produce is more affordable, fresher, and tastier.

Understanding Nutrition

A balanced diet includes a variety of foods to provide the nutrients your body needs. Aim to fill half your plate with fruits and vegetables, which are packed with vitamins, minerals, and fiber. Include lean proteins like chicken, fish, beans, and nuts, which are essential for muscle repair and overall health. Whole grains like brown rice, quinoa, and whole-wheat bread provide energy and help keep you full longer. Don't forget dairy or dairy alternatives for calcium and vitamin D, crucial for bone health.

Understanding portion sizes is key to maintaining a balanced diet. Here's how to visualize the appropriate amounts of different types of food:

Fruits and Vegetables: Fill half your plate with a variety of colorful fruits and vegetables. These should be the largest portion on your plate, as they are low in calories but high in essential nutrients like vitamins, minerals, and fiber.

Lean Proteins: About a quarter of your plate should be lean proteins. These are crucial for muscle repair and overall health. A serving size of protein, such as chicken, fish, or beans, should be about the size of your palm or a deck of cards. Nuts and seeds, which are also good protein sources, can be measured in small handfuls.

Whole Grains: Another quarter of your plate should be dedicated to whole grains. These provide long-lasting energy and help keep you full.

Dairy or Dairy Alternatives: Dairy products or fortified alternatives should be included for calcium and vitamin D, crucial for bone health.

Healthy eating plate. Infographic chart with balanced nutrition proportions.

Reading and Understanding Food Labels

Navigating food labels can sometimes feel like decoding a secret language, but they're actually a powerful tool for making healthier choices. Let's take a closer look at the food label in the image to break down the key components.

First, start by checking the **serving size** at the top of the label. This tells you the amount of food that all the nutritional information is based on. In this example, the serving size is 1 cup (230g), and there are 6 servings per container. Understanding the serving size is crucial because it helps you calculate how much of each nutrient you're actually consuming. If you eat more than the serving size, you'll need to multiply the nutritional values accordingly.

Next, take a look at the **calories** listed per serving. Calories give you an idea of how much energy you'll get from one serving of the food. In this case, 1 cup provides 245 calories. Keeping track of your caloric intake is important for maintaining a balanced diet and reaching your personal health goals.

Moving down the label, you'll see a breakdown of **macronutrients** like **Total Fat, Saturated Fat, Trans Fat, Cholesterol, Sodium, Total Carbohydrate, and Protein**. These are essential to monitor:

- **Total Fat**: This includes all types of fat in the food. Here, it's 12g per serving. Aim for foods with healthy fats, and be cautious with saturated fats and trans fats, which can increase your risk of heart disease.

- **Saturated Fat**: At 2g per serving (10% of your daily value), it's important to limit this to avoid raising LDL cholesterol levels.
- **Cholesterol and Sodium**: These can contribute to heart disease and high blood pressure if consumed in excess, so it's wise to keep an eye on them.
- **Total Carbohydrate**: Carbs are your body's main source of energy. This includes fiber (7g) and sugars (5g). High fiber content is beneficial as it aids digestion and helps you feel full longer.

Pay special attention to the **Dietary Fiber** listed. With 7g per serving, that's 25% of your daily recommended intake—a good amount to keep you full and support healthy digestion.

Below the macronutrients, you'll find **Vitamin D, Calcium, Iron, and Potassium**. These micronutrients are vital for various body functions. For example, calcium supports bone health, while iron is essential for carrying oxygen in the blood. Checking these values helps ensure you're meeting your nutritional needs.

Finally, don't skip the **ingredient list**. Ingredients are listed in descending order by weight, meaning the first few ingredients are the most prevalent in the product. Look for whole foods at the top of the list, such as whole grains or vegetables. Be cautious of ingredients like sugars and unhealthy fats listed early, as these indicate that the product is less healthy.

Understanding food labels empowers you to make informed decisions about what you're putting into your body. By paying attention to serving sizes, calorie counts, and the balance of nutrients, you can better manage your diet and ensure you're fueling your body with what it needs.

Nutrition Facts

6 servings per container

Serving size   **1 cup (230g)**

Amount per serving

Calories   245

	% Daily Value*
Total Fat 12g	**14%**
Saturated Fat 2g	**10%**
Trans Fat 0g	
Cholesterol 8mg	**3%**
Sodium 210mg	**9%**
Total Carbohydrate 34g	**12%**
Dietary Fiber 7g	**25%**
Total Sugars 5g	
Includes 4g Added Sugars	**8%**
Protein 11g	
Vitamin D 4mcg	20%
Calcium 210mg	16%
Iron 3mg	15%
Potassium 380mg	8%

*The % Daily Value (DV) tells you how much a nutrient in a serving of food contributes to a daily diet. 2,000 calories a day is used for general nutrition advice.

Nutrition facts Label.

Chapter 7: Self-Care and Mental Health

The Importance of Self-Care

Taking care of yourself is essential for maintaining both mental and physical health. In our fast-paced world, it's easy to forget to prioritize self-care, but doing so can significantly improve your overall well-being. Self-care isn't just about treating yourself to a spa day or indulging in your favorite treats—it's about integrating practices into your daily routine that nurture your body, mind, and spirit.

Daily Self-Care Routines

Creating a daily self-care routine doesn't have to be complicated. The key is to find what works best for you and your lifestyle. Here's how you can tailor self-care practices to suit different personalities and lifestyles:

Morning Rituals for Every Personality

Begin your day with intention. If you're an early riser who

loves quiet time, consider starting your day with a few minutes of meditation or journaling. This could involve sitting quietly with a cup of tea or coffee, reflecting on your goals for the day, or simply enjoying the stillness before the hustle begins. If you're someone who prefers to hit the ground running, try incorporating a short, energizing workout or a brisk walk to wake up your body and mind.

For those who thrive on creativity, consider spending your mornings engaged in a creative activity—like sketching, writing, or even just doodling. This sets a positive tone for the day and can help get your creative juices flowing.

Healthy Eating for Different Lifestyles

Fueling your body with nutritious foods is a fundamental part of self-care. If you're always on the go, meal prepping on weekends can save you time during the week and ensure you have balanced meals ready to eat. For those who enjoy cooking, try experimenting with new recipes that include a variety of fruits, vegetables, lean proteins, and whole grains. Eating well doesn't have to be boring—explore different cuisines and flavors to keep things interesting.

If you're someone who struggles with maintaining a balanced diet, consider keeping healthy snacks like nuts, fruit, or yogurt within reach. This way, you're more likely to make healthier choices throughout the day.

Physical Activity Tailored to Your Preferences

Incorporating physical activity into your day is essential for reducing stress and boosting your mood. But physical activity doesn't have to mean hitting the gym for an intense workout—find what works for you.

If you enjoy being outdoors, take advantage of nature by going for a hike, a run, or even just a walk around your neighborhood. If you're more of a social person, consider joining a group fitness class or playing a team sport. For those who prefer a more solitary approach, yoga, pilates, or even dancing in your living room can be great ways to stay active.

Remember, the goal is to move your body in a way that feels good to you. It's less about sticking to a strict regimen and more about finding joy in movement.

Evening Wind Down for a Restful Night

Your bedtime routine plays a crucial role in ensuring a good night's sleep. If you're someone who tends to have a lot on their mind at night, consider incorporating relaxation techniques like deep breathing exercises or a warm bath to help you unwind.

For book lovers, reading a few chapters of a novel before bed can be a relaxing way to disconnect from screens and ease into sleep. If you're more auditory, listening to calming music or a sleep meditation can help you drift off.

For those who struggle with anxiety or restless thoughts, practicing gentle yoga or stretching before bed can help release tension and prepare your body for rest.

Mindfulness and Meditation Techniques

Mindfulness and meditation are powerful tools for self-care that help you stay grounded in the present moment and reduce stress and anxiety. The beauty of mindfulness is that it can be adapted to fit your lifestyle, no matter how busy or relaxed it might be.

Breathing Exercises for Instant Calm

Breathing exercises are a simple and effective way to calm your nervous system, and they can be done anywhere, anytime. The 4-7-8 technique—where you inhale for four seconds, hold for seven seconds, and exhale for eight seconds—is a great way to quickly reduce stress. Whether you're at work, stuck in traffic, or about to face a challenging situation, this technique can help you regain your composure.

For those who need something even simpler, try taking a few deep breaths, focusing on the sensation of the air entering and leaving your body. Even this small act of mindfulness can make a big difference in your day.

Body Scan Meditation for Deep Relaxation

Body scan meditation is a practice where you focus on different parts of your body, from your toes to your head, noticing any tension and releasing it. This technique is particularly beneficial for those who carry stress in their bodies, as it helps you connect with and relax your physical self.

You can practice a body scan meditation lying down before sleep, during a break at work, or anytime you feel the need to relax deeply. For those who prefer a more structured approach, guided body scan meditations are available online and through several meditation apps, which will help lead you through the process.

Mindful Walking for Presence and Peace

Mindful walking is an excellent way to combine physical activity with mindfulness. As you walk, focus on the sights, sounds, and sensations around you. Notice the feeling of the ground beneath your feet, the rhythm of your breath, and the sounds of nature or city life.

This practice is perfect for those who find it hard to sit still for traditional meditation. It allows you to be present in the moment while also moving your body. Whether you're walking to work, strolling through a park, or even just pacing around your home, mindful walking can be a calming and centering practice.

By tailoring these self-care routines and mindfulness practices to your lifestyle and personality, you can create a daily routine that truly nurtures your body, mind, and spirit. Remember, self-care is not a one-size-fits-all approach—find what resonates with you and make it a regular part of your life.

Managing Stress and Anxiety

Stress and anxiety are common experiences, but recognizing and managing them effectively is key to maintaining mental health.

Recognizing Signs of Burnout and Stress

Burnout and stress can creep up on you, often without you even realizing it. Signs of burnout include chronic fatigue, irritability, difficulty concentrating, and a lack of motivation. Stress can manifest as headaches, muscle tension, sleep disturbances, and digestive issues.

- **Listen to Your Body**: Pay attention to physical symptoms like headaches, muscle tension, and changes in sleep patterns. These can be early warning signs of stress.
- **Emotional Signals**: Notice if you're feeling more irritable, anxious, or overwhelmed than usual. Emotional changes often indicate that you're reaching your limit.

Techniques for Managing Stress and Anxiety

Once you recognize the signs of stress and anxiety, it's crucial to take proactive steps to manage them effectively. Managing stress and anxiety isn't about eliminating them entirely—that's often impossible—but rather about learning how to navigate through them in a way that minimizes their impact on your life.

66

Here are some additional techniques that can help:

Cognitive Behavioral Techniques: Cognitive Behavioral Therapy (CBT) strategies are designed to help you reframe negative thoughts that contribute to stress and anxiety. One effective technique is cognitive restructuring, where you challenge and replace negative or distorted thoughts with more balanced, realistic ones. For example, if you're feeling overwhelmed by a work project, instead of thinking, "I'll never get this done," you can reframe it to, "I can take this one step at a time and ask for help if I need it." Over time, practicing this can change the way you perceive stressors, making them feel more manageable.

Journaling: Writing down your thoughts and feelings can be a powerful way to manage stress and anxiety. Journaling allows you to process emotions, identify triggers, and track patterns in your stress levels over time. It's also a great way to practice gratitude, which has been shown to reduce anxiety by shifting your focus to positive aspects of your life. Setting aside just 10-15 minutes a day to write in a journal can help you gain clarity and perspective, which can alleviate the intensity of stress and anxiety.

Creating a Balanced Routine: Establishing a routine that includes time for work, rest, and play is essential for managing stress. A balanced routine helps prevent burnout by ensuring you have time to recharge. Incorporate activities that bring you joy, whether it's reading, gardening, or spending time with loved ones. Having a routine that you enjoy can act as a buffer against the pressures of daily life.

Sensory Grounding Techniques: When anxiety starts to feel overwhelming, grounding techniques can help bring you back to the present moment. One method is the 5-4-3-2-1 technique, where you identify five things you can see, four things you can touch, three things you can hear, two things you can smell, and one thing you can taste. This sensory exercise shifts your focus away from anxious thoughts and helps you reconnect with the here and now, reducing the intensity of anxiety.

Hobbies and Creative Outlets: Engaging in hobbies or creative activities can provide a healthy escape from stress. Whether it's painting, playing a musical instrument, crafting, or writing, these activities allow you to express yourself and take your mind off your worries. Creative outlets can also serve as a form of therapy, providing relief from anxiety by channeling your energy into something positive and productive.

Healthy Sleep Habits: Stress and anxiety often interfere with sleep, creating a vicious cycle. Developing good sleep hygiene can improve your ability to cope with stress. This includes setting a regular sleep schedule, creating a calming bedtime routine, and minimizing exposure to screens before bed. Ensuring you get enough restful sleep can significantly reduce your stress levels and help you face challenges with a clearer mind.

Limiting Stimulants: Caffeine, nicotine, and other stimulants can exacerbate anxiety and disrupt sleep patterns. While it's tempting to rely on coffee or energy drinks to power through stressful days, they can actually heighten feelings of anxiety. Consider reducing your intake of these substances or switching to calming alternatives like herbal teas.

By incorporating these techniques into your daily life, you can build resilience against stress and anxiety. Remember, managing stress is an ongoing process, and it's okay to try different strategies to find what works best for you. The goal isn't to eliminate stress altogether but to develop a toolkit of techniques that help you navigate life's challenges with greater ease and confidence.

Giving Yourself Grace

In our quest for success and perfection, we often forget to be kind to ourselves. We push ourselves to the limit, striving for excellence, and sometimes lose sight of the importance of self-compassion. Giving yourself grace means recognizing your efforts, accepting your imperfections, and treating yourself with the same kindness you'd offer to a friend. Understanding the importance of giving yourself grace can lead to a healthier and more balanced life.

Understanding Perfectionism and Its Pitfalls

Perfectionism can be a double-edged sword. On one hand, it can drive you to achieve great things and reach high standards. On the other hand, an obsession with perfection can lead to chronic stress, anxiety, and burnout. It's important to know when your drive for perfection is helping you and when it's hurting you.

Set Realistic Goals: Aim for progress, not perfection. It's great to have high standards, but make sure your goals are achievable. Understand that making mistakes is a natural part of the learning process. For example, if you're learning a new skill like playing the guitar, don't expect to master it overnight. Celebrate the small milestones, like learning a new chord or playing a simple song. These moments of progress are what truly matter.

Self-Compassion: Treat yourself with the same kindness and understanding that you would offer to a friend. Imagine your friend is feeling down because they didn't get a perfect score on a test. You'd probably tell them it's okay and remind them of all the hard work they put in. Do the same for yourself. Remember, everyone has flaws, and that's what makes us human. It's okay to be imperfect.

Reflect on Your Reactions: Think about times when you've been too hard on yourself. Maybe you didn't get the grade you wanted on a project or forgot an important task at work. Instead of beating yourself up, take a step back and look at the bigger picture. Did you do your best? Did you learn something from the experience? If the answer is yes, then give yourself some credit.

Giving yourself grace also means taking breaks and not pushing yourself too hard. If you're exhausted, it's okay to rest. If you're feeling overwhelmed, it's okay to take a step back and prioritize your mental health. Sometimes, the best way to achieve your goals is to give yourself the time and space to recharge.

Learning to Forgive Yourself and Celebrate Small Wins

Forgiving yourself for mistakes and celebrating your achieve-ments, no matter how small, are essential aspects of self-care. This is one of my personal favorite tips because it's all about being kind to yourself and recognizing the value in every step forward, no matter how tiny it might seem. Celebrating small wins not only makes you feel good but also encourages positive behavior. It's like giving yourself a high-five and saying, "You did it!" This helps build momentum and keeps you motivated to continue.

Reflect and Learn: When you make a mistake, take a moment to reflect on it. Think about what went wrong and what you can learn from the experience. Instead of beating yourself up, use it as an opportunity for growth. For example, if you missed a deadline at work, consider what factors contributed to it and how you can manage your time better in the future. Mistakes are valuable lessons in disguise.

Acknowledge Your Progress: Celebrate your accomplishments, no matter how small they are. This could be anything from finishing a project to maintaining a new habit, or even just making it through a tough day. Treat yourself to something you enjoy. Here are a few ways you can celebrate or treat yourself:

- **Indulge in Your Favorite Activity**: Spend an evening watch-ing your favorite movie or TV show, playing a video game, or reading a book you've been wanting to dive into.
- **Pamper Yourself**: Treat yourself to a relaxing bath with your favorite bath salts and a good book, or perhaps enjoy a

special treat like a fancy coffee or dessert from your favorite bakery.

· **Share Your Wins**: Sometimes, sharing your accomplishments with friends or family can make them even more meaningful. Call a friend, send a text, or make a social media post about what you've achieved. Their positive responses can amplify your own feelings of pride and satisfaction.

Chapter 8: Co-Working and Teamwork

Effective Collaboration

Working effectively in a team can be a game-changer. It's like being part of a sports team—each player has a role, and together, you aim for victory. Being a team player means understanding that everyone's contribution matters. Think of it as building a puzzle: each piece is unique, but they all fit together to create the big picture.

How to work effectively in a team

Know Your Role: Understand your responsibilities and how they fit into the team's goals. If you're unsure, don't hesitate to ask for clarification. Clear roles help avoid stepping on each other's toes.

Be Open to Others' Ideas: Everyone brings something different to the table. Listening to others' suggestions can spark new ideas and lead to better solutions. For example, during a group project, someone might suggest an idea you hadn't thought of—this could be the missing piece to your puzzle.

Stay Positive and Supportive: Encourage your teammates. A positive attitude boosts morale and makes working together more enjoyable. Celebrate each other's successes and provide support when someone faces challenges. It's like being a cheerleader for your team, keeping everyone motivated and focused.

Communication skills for better collaboration

Good communication is the backbone of effective teamwork. It's the glue that holds the team together. Active listening is a vital part of this. Pay attention when your teammates are speaking and show that you value their input by nodding or giving verbal feedback. Improving your listening skills can make a huge difference in team dynamics as this helps build trust and ensures everyone feels heard.

When sharing your ideas, be clear and concise. Avoid jargon and keep it simple. This makes it easier for everyone to understand and follow along. For example, in a group project, explaining your point in clear terms helps everyone get on the same page quickly, avoiding confusion and saving time.

Don't be afraid to ask questions if you're unclear about something. Questions can clarify misunderstandings and ensure everyone is on the same page. If you're working on a group project and don't understand a part of it, asking questions can help you get the clarity you need to contribute effectively. I once worked on a tech project where jargon flew over my head. Asking questions not only helped me understand but also showed my team I was engaged and eager to learn.

Offloading and Delegation

Delegation isn't just about handing off work—it's about empowering your team and ensuring tasks are completed efficiently. Strategic delegation can be crucial for effective teamwork and helps prevent burnout.

- **Learning to Delegate Tasks:** Assign tasks based on your teammates' strengths and skills. If someone is great at research, let them handle that part of the project. This ensures the task is done well and efficiently. Richard Branson, founder of Virgin Group, advises, "If you really want to grow as an entrepreneur, you've got to learn to delegate." Finding the right person for the job is key to effective delegation.
- **Provide Clear Instructions:** When delegating, provide clear and detailed instructions. Explain the task, its goals, and any deadlines. This helps prevent confusion and ensures the task is completed correctly. A clear set of instructions can make the difference between success and frustration.

Trusting others to share the load

Build Trust Gradually: Trusting your teammates is essential for effective delegation. It's about believing in their abilities and supporting them as they take on new responsibilities. Start by delegating smaller tasks and gradually increase the complexity as your trust grows. This helps both you and your teammates feel more comfortable with the delegation process. When I started delegating tasks, I began with simple assignments. Over time, as trust grew, I handed over more complex tasks, which boosted team confidence and efficiency.

Offer Support: Providing support is a crucial part of effective leadership. Be available to answer questions and provide guidance. Let your teammates know they can come to you if they need help. This builds a supportive environment where everyone feels confident in their roles.

Acknowledge Efforts and Successes: Recognize and appreciate your teammates' hard work. This boosts their confidence and reinforces the positive effects of delegation. When someone completes a task well, acknowledge their effort. It creates a positive feedback loop that encourages more great work.

Chapter 9: Building Relationships

Maintaining Friendships

As we navigate life's ups and downs, friendships provide a vital support system. Friends offer advice, lend a listening ear, or simply share a laugh when you need it most. According to psychologist Dr. Julianne Holt-Lunstad, having strong social connections can improve your overall well-being and even increase your lifespan. Friendships help reduce stress, combat loneliness, and boost happiness.

The importance of friendships in adulthood

Friendships in adulthood are crucial because they offer emotional support and companionship. They help you feel understood and valued, which is essential for your mental health. Friends are the ones who cheer you on during your successes and offer comfort during tough times. They are the people you can be yourself with, without fear of judgment.

Moreover, friendships provide different perspectives and insights, helping you navigate challenges and make better decisions. Whether it's discussing career moves, personal dilemmas, or getting advice on everyday matters, having friends to talk to can be incredibly beneficial. This sense of belonging and acceptance can significantly enhance your quality of life by lowering stress levels, reducing the risk of depression, and even improving immune function.

In adulthood, making time for friends can be challenging due to busy schedules and responsibilities, but it's essential to prioritize these relationships. Strong friendships are built on mutual respect, trust, and understanding. They require effort, but the rewards—emotional support, shared joy, and a sense of community—are well worth it.

Tips for maintaining and strengthening relationships

Investing in friendships involves more than just occasional socializing; it means being there for each other consistently. It involves sharing experiences, celebrating each other's milestones, and providing support during difficult times. By nurturing these bonds, you not only enrich your own life but also contribute positively to the lives of your friends.

Here are some tips to keep your friendships strong and vibrant:

1. **Regular Check-ins**: Life gets busy, but a quick text or call can keep the connection alive. Even if it's just to say, "Hey, thinking about you!" it shows you care.
2. **Make Time for Each Other**: Schedule regular hangouts,

whether it's a monthly coffee date or a weekly game night. Having something to look forward to can keep the friendship thriving.

3. **Be a Good Listener**: Show genuine interest in your friends' lives. Listen to their problems and celebrate their successes. Sometimes, just being there to listen is the most supportive thing you can do. Remember, friendships are a two-way street.

4. **Be Honest and Open**: If something's bothering you, communicate it. Honest conversations can prevent misunderstandings and strengthen your bond.

5. **Celebrate Milestones**: Celebrate each other's achievements and milestones, no matter how big or small. Whether it's a birthday, a job promotion, or finishing a tough project, celebrating together creates lasting memories.

Making New Friends as an Adult

Making new friends as an adult can feel like a daunting task. Unlike in school, where you're surrounded by peers every day, adult life doesn't always offer the same opportunities to meet new people. However, building new friendships is possible and can be incredibly rewarding, offering fresh perspectives and enriching your life.

One of the most important things to remember when making new friends as an adult is to be open and proactive. You might not stumble upon friendships as easily as you did in childhood, but with a bit of effort, you can form meaningful connections.

Start with Common Interests

A great way to meet new people is by pursuing activities that you enjoy. Whether it's joining a local sports league, attending a book club, or taking a cooking class, these settings provide natural opportunities to connect with others who share your interests. When you're doing something you love, it's easier to strike up conversations and bond over shared experiences.

For example, if you're passionate about fitness, consider joining a gym or participating in group exercise classes. Not only will you stay active, but you'll also have the chance to meet people who value a healthy lifestyle, just like you.

Don't Be Afraid to Make the First Move

In adulthood, everyone's busy with their own lives, so sometimes you have to be the one to reach out. Don't be afraid to take the initiative. If you meet someone at work, at a social event, or even online who you'd like to get to know better, suggest grabbing a coffee or attending a local event together. Most people appreciate the effort and are likely open to making new friends too.

Remember, it's okay to feel a little awkward at first. Building a new friendship takes time, and it's normal to feel nervous when reaching out to someone new. But by taking that first step, you're opening the door to a potential new connection.

Leverage Your Existing Network

Sometimes, the best way to make new friends is through the people you already know. Ask your current friends, family members, or colleagues to introduce you to others who share your interests. Attending gatherings or events where you know only a few people can also expand your circle and help you meet new friends.

For instance, if a friend invites you to a party where you don't know many people, go with an open mind and a willingness to engage. You never know—one of their friends could become your friend too.

Join Online Communities

In today's digital age, online communities offer a great way to meet new people, especially if you're interested in niche hobbies or topics. Platforms like Meetup, Facebook groups, or even Reddit offer countless communities where you can connect with others who share your interests.

Joining these groups can lead to both online and in-person friendships. Whether you're discussing your favorite books, sharing recipes, or planning local meetups, online communities can be a gateway to real-world connections.

Be Patient and Persistent

Building new friendships takes time. It's important to be patient and not get discouraged if connections don't happen immediately. Just like any relationship, friendships need to be nurtured and allowed to grow naturally.

Keep putting yourself out there, and eventually, you'll find people who click with you. Even if it takes a little time, the friendships you build will be worth the effort.

Making new friends as an adult might require stepping out of your comfort zone, but it's an essential part of creating a fulfilling and balanced life. By being open, proactive, and patient, you can form meaningful connections that bring joy and support to your life.

Navigating Romantic Relationships

Romantic relationships add another layer of complexity and joy to our lives. They bring unique challenges and immense fulfillment, requiring effort, understanding, and balance. In the context of this book, which aims to equip you with essential life skills for adulting, understanding how to maintain healthy romantic relationships is crucial. These relationships are not just about finding love but about growing as individuals and as partners, supporting each other's goals, and building a life together. Let's dive into the essentials of maintaining healthy romantic relationships and balancing personal growth with partnership.

Healthy communication in romantic relationships

Communication is the foundation of any strong relationship. It's about expressing your thoughts and feelings openly and honestly while also being a good listener. Effective communication helps partners understand each other better, resolve conflicts, and build a stronger emotional connection.

In a romantic relationship, open communication means sharing your fears, dreams, and expectations. It's important to be transparent about your needs and listen actively to your partner's. This mutual exchange fosters trust and intimacy. According to relationship expert Dr. John Gottman, "Couples who engage in healthy communication are more likely to resolve conflicts effectively and build a stronger emotional bond." Healthy communication can prevent misunderstandings and ensure that both partners feel valued and heard.

For example, discussing your future goals and how they align can help you both understand each other's aspirations and find common ground. If one partner wants to travel the world while the other dreams of buying a house, talking about these goals can help you find a compromise that satisfies both desires. This kind of dialogue is essential for maintaining harmony and ensuring that both partners are on the same page.

Empathy and validation are also key components of healthy communication. When your partner expresses something, even if you don't fully understand or agree, acknowledging their perspective shows that you respect and care about their emotions. This validation can strengthen your connection and make your partner feel more secure in the relationship.

Remember, communication isn't just about talking; it's also about listening. Pay attention to non-verbal cues like body language and facial expressions. These can often convey more than words and help you understand your partner's true feelings. By being a good listener, you show your partner that you value their thoughts and feelings, which is fundamental to any healthy relationship.

Incorporating these communication skills into your romantic relationships can enhance your connection and help you navigate the complexities of adult life with a supportive partner by your side. As you continue to develop these skills, you'll find that they not only improve your romantic relationships but also contribute to your overall personal growth and well-being.

Balancing personal growth and partnership

Balancing your personal growth with your relationship can be challenging but rewarding. It's about supporting each other's individual goals while nurturing your bond as a couple.

Pursue Your Passions: Encourage each other to pursue individual interests and hobbies. Supporting one another in these passions keeps you both fulfilled and brings fresh energy into the relationship, adding excitement and creating a sense of balance.

Set Shared Goals: While individual growth is important, setting goals together is equally vital. Whether it's planning a trip, saving for a house, or starting a new hobby as a couple, having shared goals strengthens your partnership.

Maintain Independence: It's healthy to have your own space and time apart. Maintaining independence ensures you both have the freedom to grow individually while appreciating the time you spend together.

Support Each Other: Be each other's biggest cheerleader. Celebrate successes and provide comfort during tough times. Supporting each other's growth fosters a strong and resilient relationship.

Building and maintaining strong relationships—both friendships and romantic partnerships—requires effort, communication, and mutual respect. By investing in these relationships, you create a supportive network that enriches your life and helps you navigate its challenges and joys. So, reach out, connect, and cherish the bonds you build—they're the foundation of a fulfilling and happy life.

Conclusion

As we wrap up this journey through essential life skills for adulting, it's time to reflect on what you've learned. Take a moment to look back on everything you've accomplished so far. Reflecting on your journey helps you see how far you've come and what you've learned along the way. It's important to recognize your growth and the challenges you've overcome. This reflection isn't just about patting yourself on the back—it's about understanding your strengths and identifying areas for further improvement.

Think about the new skills you've gained, from mastering basic cooking to managing your finances. Recall the times you've successfully navigated stressful situations or effectively communicated in your relationships. These moments are milestones on your journey to becoming a more capable and confident adult.

Dr. Carol Dweck, a renowned psychologist, emphasizes the power of a growth mindset. She says, "The view you adopt for yourself profoundly affects the way you lead your life." By reflecting on your progress, you're embracing a growth mindset, recognizing that you can always learn and improve.

With a clear understanding of where you've been, it's time to set goals for where you want to go. Setting goals provides direction and motivation. These goals don't have to be monumental—small, achievable steps are just as important. They keep you moving forward and help build momentum.

Start by considering what you want to achieve in the next few months. Maybe you want to improve your time management, enhance your cooking skills, or deepen your friendships. Write down your goals and make a plan for how you'll achieve them. Break them down into smaller, manageable steps.

Remember, goals can change. Life is unpredictable, and it's okay to adjust your goals as you go. The important thing is to keep aiming for improvement. As life coach Tony Robbins says, "Setting goals is the first step in turning the invisible into the visible."

You now have a roadmap to success. Adulthood is a continuous journey of learning and growth. Embrace the idea of lifelong learning—whether it's picking up a new hobby, taking a course, or simply staying curious about the world around you. Each new skill you acquire adds to your toolkit and helps you handle life's challenges more effectively.

Lifelong learning keeps your mind sharp and your life exciting. It helps you adapt to changes and stay resilient in the face of setbacks. By staying curious and open to new experiences, you build the resilience needed to thrive in adulthood.

Life is full of ups and downs, and adulthood is no different. There will be moments of triumph and moments of failure. The key is to embrace both. Understand that setbacks are a natural part of life and an opportunity to learn and grow. When things don't go as planned, take a deep breath, reflect on what happened, and consider what you can do differently next time.

Having a supportive network of friends and family can make navigating these ups and downs easier. Lean on them when you need support, and be there for them in return. Together, you can weather any storm.

Remember, you're not alone on this journey. Every adult faces challenges and makes mistakes. What matters is how you respond to those challenges and what you learn from them. As Dr. Seuss wisely said, "You have brains in your head. You have feet in your shoes. You can steer yourself any direction you choose."

As we bring it all together, it's important to reflect on the journey we've taken through this book—especially if you deal with anxiety or identify as neurodiverse. These challenges might make the road ahead feel more complex, but they also provide you with unique strengths and perspectives that can guide you toward a fulfilling adult life.

Throughout this book, you've gained valuable skills and insights tailored to your specific needs. Whether it's managing stress and anxiety, developing effective time management strategies, or building supportive relationships, each lesson has been designed to help you navigate the complexities of adulthood with greater ease. Now, it's time to put these lessons into practice.

Your path to success might not look like everyone else's—and that's okay. Your journey is unique, and the strategies you've learned here are tools to help you thrive in your own way. Reflect on the techniques that resonated with you, whether it's breaking tasks into smaller steps, using mindfulness to stay grounded, or finding creative outlets for self-expression.

Setting future goals is a powerful way to keep moving forward, but don't forget to give yourself grace along the way. Progress is progress, no matter how small it may seem. Continuously improving and embracing both the ups and downs are key to building resilience. And remember, setbacks aren't failures—they're opportunities to learn, adapt, and grow stronger.

The path to success isn't a straight line; for most of us, it feels more like a winding road with unexpected turns. But each twist and turn is part of your journey, filled with learning experiences, growth opportunities, and moments of joy. Embrace it all, knowing that the skills and strategies you've gained from this book are your companions along the way. As you continue to learn and grow, use these tools to build a life that reflects your values, supports your mental and emotional health, and celebrates your unique strengths. Adulthood may have its challenges, but with confidence and resilience, you can navigate it with grace and emerge stronger on the other side. You've got this!

Notes

Chapter 1: Embracing Independence

Leaving the Nest

   1. Pew Research Center. (2020). "A Third of Young Adults Live at Home, Highest Level Since Great Depression."

Coping with the Fear of Leaving Home

   2. Pew Research Center. (2020). "A Third of Young Adults Live at Home, Highest Level Since Great Depression."

Chapter 2: Financial Literacy

Basic Budgeting: The Magic of Planning

   3. Sethi, Ramit. "I Will Teach You to Be Rich."

Chapter 4: Workplace Confidence

Navigating Workplace Anxiety

   4. American Psychological Association. "Exercise and Stress: Get Moving to Manage Stress."

   5. Brown, Dr. Brené. "The Power of Vulnerability."

Decision Making

   6. Gladwell, Malcolm. "Blink: The Power of Thinking Without

Thinking."

Growth Mindset, Self-Confidence, and Resilience
7. Dweck, Dr. Carol. *"Mindset: The New Psychology of Success."*

Chapter 5: Neurodiversity and Learning

Understanding Neurodiverse Learning Complications
8. Brown, Dr. Thomas E. *"A New Understanding of ADHD in Children and Adults: Executive Function Impairments."*

Chapter 7: Self-Care and Mental Health

Mindfulness and Meditation Techniques
9. Kabat-Zinn, Jon. *"Wherever You Go, There You Are: Mindfulness Meditation in Everyday Life."*

Giving Yourself Grace
10. Dweck, Dr. Carol. *"Mindset: The New Psychology of Success."*
11. Robbins, Tony. *"Awaken the Giant Within."*

Chapter 8: Co-Working and Teamwork

Offloading and Delegation
12. Branson, Richard. *"Like a Virgin: Secrets They Won't Teach You at Business School."*

Chapter 9: Building Relationships

Maintaining Friendships
13. Holt-Lunstad, Dr. Julianne. *"The Importance of Social*

Relationships to Health."

Navigating Romantic Relationships

14. Gottman, Dr. John. *"The Seven Principles for Making Marriage Work."*

Conclusion

Setting Goals for the Future

15. Jobs, Steve. *Commencement address, Stanford University, 2005.*

16. Robbins, Tony. *"Awaken the Giant Within."*

Embracing the Ups and Downs of Adulthood

17. Seuss, Dr. *"Oh, the Places You'll Go!"*

Share Your Feedback

Thank you for taking the time to read this book!

Your thoughts mean a lot to me, and if this guide has been helpful to you, I would truly appreciate it if you could take a moment to share a positive review on Amazon. Simply scan the QR code below to head over to the review page. Your feedback not only supports me but also helps others who might benefit from the book as well.

If you have any concerns or constructive feedback, I'd love to hear from you directly—please feel free to email me at **whiteincbooks@gmail.com** so I can continue improving and providing the best possible resources for readers like you.

Thank you for being a part of this journey!

Made in the USA
Coppell, TX
29 December 2024

43514490R00056